A Capital City System

Stephen Lockwood
Series editor Robert J Harley

MP **Middleton Press**

Cover Photograph: *Fifty of these BUT double-deckers, which replaced the last of Cardiff's trams between 1948 and 1950, formed the backbone of the city's trolleybus fleet. The body design featured a rear entrance, forward-exit doorway and two staircases. The exit door became disused following the demise of the pay as you enter flat fare scheme and most were subsequently removed. This vehicle, 262, was purchased for preservation upon withdrawal in 1968 and had its doorway re-instated. It is seen at Victoria Park in 1969 operating on an enthusiasts' tour looking very much as it did when it was brand new in 1949. (R.Marshall/Photobus)*

> **Deffro maen ddydd, Y Ddraig Goch ddyry cychwyn**
>
> **(Awake, it is day! The Red Dragon will lead the way)**

The motto included in the City of Cardiff coat of arms,
as carried on the city's trolleybuses.

Published August 2005

ISBN 1 904474 64 0

© *Middleton Press, 2005*

Design Deborah Esher

Published by
  Middleton Press
  Easebourne Lane
  Midhurst, West Sussex
  GU29 9AZ
Tel: 01730 813169
Fax: 01730 812601
Email: info@middletonpress.co.uk
www.middletonpress.co.uk

Printed & bound by Biddles Ltd, Kings Lynn

CONTENTS

INTRODUCTION AND ACKNOWLEDGEMENTS

Cardiff was one of the last places in Britain to commence trolleybus operation. Most British systems had been established by 1939, but Cardiff's first route opened in the middle of the Second World War. Only Glasgow commenced trolleybus operation later than this – in 1949. By this time, Cardiff had replaced most of its trams with trolleybuses, a process that was completed in 1950. A further and final major extension took place in 1955, when the system peaked at 79 vehicles and 18 route miles. The fleet was comprised entirely of six-wheelers, a situation shared only with the Huddersfield system, and included some single-deckers, necessary to negotiate a route with a very low bridge. By the time the operation closed in 1970, leaving only three other systems still in existence, Cardiff's six-wheelers were the last of this type left in public service in Britain.

I came to know Cardiff's trolleybuses during the last years of the system, but fortunately when there were four routes still in operation, and the imposing crimson lake liveried vehicles still glided along St Mary Street, Duke Street and, by that time, alongside the City Hall.

This publication is essentially a route-by-route pictorial album. It is aimed at bringing back memories to those who knew the vehicles or to give a flavour of what it was like to those who never knew Cardiff during the trolleybus era. It is not intended as a definitive history as there have been excellent historical books in the past on both the trolleybus and tram systems.

Many individuals have provided assistance with the preparation of this book. I am grateful to all those photographers who so willingly supplied or loaned prints and allowed their work to be shown here. They are individually credited in the photograph captions. Special mention needs to be made to three transport preservation organisations that played a major role in the provision of photographs. The Cardiff Transport Preservation Group, through its chairman Mike Taylor, has made available to me the Cardiff trolleybus photograph collection owned by Mike's father, Chris Taylor. Copies from the collection are available to purchase from the Group (www.ctpg.co.uk). The National Trolleybus Association, who hold much of the Bob Mack trolleybus negative collection, made special arrangements through Robin Hellyar-Symonds and David Hall to digitise the extensive Cardiff section of this for the book. The Ipswich Transport Museum photograph collection yielded some interesting views which were discovered by fellow Middleton Press author Colin Barker during his own researches. Much additional archive material has been supplied by Eric Old, Peter Smith and Chris Taylor. Paul Watson has once again produced excellent prints from some elderly negatives. Thanks go to all those mentioned above.

The excellent overhead wiring maps have been kindly drawn by Roger Smith. The main map is based on one drawn by the late Keith Stretch, to which much additional information has been added. I am grateful to Peter Smith of Cardiff for assisting Roger with this and ensuring maximum accuracy.

Chris Taylor and Peter Smith have very kindly read my text and suggested additions and improvements as necessary.

Finally, loving thanks go once again to my wife Eileen, for her constant support and encourage-ment during the preparation of this book.

GEOGRAPHICAL SETTING

Cardiff, a city since 1905 and the capital city of Wales since 1955, lies in the very south of the principality, where the River Taff flows into the Bristol Channel. Ten miles or so to the north, beyond Pontypridd and Caerphilly, lie steeply sided valleys: the Rhondda, Cynon, Taff and Rhymney, which in the nineteenth and early twentieth century were the source of coal that was shipped from Cardiff all over the world. By the outbreak of the First World War the city had become the world's largest coal exporting port. At the time of the trolleybus era, Cardiff's population had grown to around 260,000. Due to the extensive network of railways crossing the city streets, there were several points on the trolleybus system where the vehicles had to squeeze under low bridges and the headroom of one of these, in Bute Street, was so low that only single-deck trolleybuses were able to pass thorough.

HISTORICAL BACKGROUND

Like the vast majority of trolleybus systems in Britain, that at Cardiff took over from an electric tramway system. In 1902, the two existing horse tramway companies had been purchased by Cardiff Corporation, and these were converted to electric traction as soon as possible. By 1928, when the electric tram system reached its peak, there were 142 cars running over 19.5 miles/31.3km of route. The operation was plagued by low railway bridges, resulting in two routes being run with single-deck bogie trams. Since 1923, 81 double-deck cars, to a special low-height design with modified trucks and small wheels, had entered service to minimise the problems of the bridges. In the 1930s, a review of the system's future took place partly due to the need to replace worn out track and to speed-up services. Both the single deck tram routes were converted to motorbuses, the Salisbury Road service in 1930, and the Grangetown to Splott route in 1936.

However, trolleybus operation had not been neglected in the Council's thoughts. Investigations had taken place into the possibilities of railless electric traction as early as 1911, and in 1919 there was a proposal to operate a feeder service with trolleybuses from the Whitchurch Road tram terminus. Eventually, the running of trolleybuses over the existing tramway network was authorised by the Cardiff Corporation Act of 1934. Nothing immediately happened as a result of this, but the chance to consider trolleybuses came towards the end of the decade when the replacement of the tram route in the Wood Street area became a priority. The management of the Transport Department, backed by the transport committee, strongly favoured replacement by motorbuses, but other factions of the Council, notably the electricity and finance committees, strongly favoured trolleybuses. No doubt the trolleybus argument was bolstered by the harsh conditions in the nearby coalfields, where unemployment and social strife were prevalent. Trolleybuses depended on electricity produced by a coal-fired power station thereby helping to alleviate the plight of the Welsh miners. Ultimately, in May 1939, the City Council instructed their transport management to 'take immediate steps' to replace the tramways with trolleybuses. The Cardiff Corporation (Trolley Vehicles) Order Confirmation Act 1940 not only confirmed the powers to run trolleybuses over the tramway system, but also authorised many other routes extending way beyond present operations. If all these routes had come to fruition, Cardiff would have ultimately had the largest trolleybus system in Britain outside London.

The outbreak of the Second World War slowed down Cardiff's trolleybus plans, and caused difficulties in the manufacture of the vehicles needed to replace trams on the No.6 Wood Street to Clarence Road service. The system eventually opened on St David's Day, 1st March 1942, and Cardiff's trolleybus era had begun. The drab AEC trolleybuses in their wartime grey paint also introduced a new fare collection scheme 'pay as you enter' (PAYE). A glass–fronted fare collection box was mounted on the platform for passengers to deposit the flat 1d fare on boarding. No tickets were issued and the conductor supervised the procedure and looked after the platform. The theory behind the scheme was that it eliminated much of the cost of fare collection, reduced fare evasion, and made the system more equable. For instance, those residents who had been moved away from the city centre by housing improvement schemes did not have to pay a higher fare. The concept was extended to the trams and some motorbus services in due course. Eventually the need to increase fares, already increased from 1d to 1½ d, creating change-giving problems, caused the scheme to be abandoned in favour of conventional fare collection by conductors from 12th November 1950.

On 8th November 1942, the existing trolleybus route was extended through the city centre, passing the Castle to the pleasant Cathedral Road area at Llandaff Fields.

Wartime conditions prevented any further trolleybus developments, mainly due to the non-availability of new vehicles of a suitable type. After the war, orders were placed with AEC and East Lancashire Coachbuilders for 75 trolleybuses (five of these being for single-deckers). These would have bodies designed jointly by the Transport Department and the coachbuilder to facilitate the PAYE system, the design incorporating two staircases and a driver operated front exit door. The chassis were built by British United Traction, successors to the AEC and Leyland trolleybus production.

Further deterioration of the tram tracks led to the urgent need to replace tram route 16 via Bute Street to Pier Head. A temporary motorbus service was substituted in April 1946 until trolleybuses could be sourced for the service. A low bridge was situated on the route that even Cardiff's low design of double deck trolleybus could not pass under (even though the low-height trams could). The solution was to purchase seven 1930 vintage single-deck trolleybuses from Pontypridd, and these entered service on the route from 17th August 1947. At the same time the original Clarence Road trolleybus route was extended a short distance along James Street, crossing the Glamorganshire Canal swing bridge, to Pier Head, the extended workings being originally allocated service number 6A.

By early 1948, the first of the new trolleybuses began to be delivered, and were at first used to allow the original AEC trolleybuses to be overhauled. After this process, the new vehicles could be used to replace the remainder of the tram services. By November 1950, when the procedure was completed, 55 new trolleybuses had entered service, including five single-deckers to oust the ex-Pontypridd veterans on the Pier Head route. Trolleybuses commenced on each route on the following dates:

5A/5B	Victoria Park to Wood Street circular	6th June 1948
5	Victoria Park to Windsor Place	4th July 1948
3	Roath Park to St Mary Street	3rd December 1949
1	Gabalfa (Whitchurch Rd) to St Mary Street	20th February 1950
2	Pengam to St Mary Street	15th October 1950

Cardiff's final tram service, to Whitchurch Road, operated for the last time on 19th February 1950, the Newport Road tram route having been temporarily converted to motorbuses in October 1948. Major work was necessary to lower the road under the Queen Street railway bridges to allow trolleybuses to operate, resulting in the remaining trams being diverted via Adam Street in July 1949. In the main, the trolleybus routes were the same as the tram routes they replaced, although a short extension was necessary, at Whitchurch Road, Gabalfa, to facilitate turning the vehicles. Other exceptions were the Newport Road service, which was extended a third of a mile beyond the tram terminus at Roath Depot into the Pengam housing area and the Clarence Road route, extended from there along James Street to Bute Street. In the city centre, trolleybuses on services 1 and 3 were routed on a one-way loop from Queen Street via a newly constructed road, Churchill Way, then via Bute Terrace, Custom House Street to St Mary Street. This proved unpopular and after just over a year the former tram routeing via St John Street and Working Street was wired for trolleybuses and used thereafter instead of Churchill Way.

In October 1951, three new cross-city trolleybus services, numbered 4, 8 and 9, commenced operation. This resulted in all trolleybus termini apart from the Bute Street service, having two services operating to it with one at least giving a direct connection to another part of the city. As no additional vehicles were involved, presumably this was achieved by reducing the frequencies of the existing services.

Consideration was now being given by the Transport Department to extending the trolleybus services. There were still un-built vehicles outstanding from the large order placed after the war. The electrical equipment for these, however, had been supplied. This was one reason why the Corporation decided to extend the wires beyond

Victoria Park into the Ely housing scheme, replacing an existing three-minute frequency motorbus service. The route had been proposed for trams in the 1920's, and indeed the main road in the area, Grand Avenue, incorporated a centre grass strip which was originally constructed to carry a reserved track tramway. Thirteen new trolleybuses were delivered and four miles of new overhead erected. The service, numbered 10A or 10B, depending which way round the large terminal loop was being operated, came into use on 8th May 1955.

The Cardiff trolleybus system was now at its maximum extent with 79 trolleybuses operating over 18 miles/29km of route. The services operated were:-

1	Gabalfa to St Mary Street
2	Pengam to St Mary Street
2A	Pengam to Victoria Park
3	Roath Park to St Mary Street
4	Roath Park to Llandaff Fields
5	Victoria Park to Windsor Lane
5A/B	Victoria Park circular via Wood Street and Castle Street
6	Llandaff Fields to Pier Head
8	Royal Oak to Victoria Park
9	Gabalfa to Pier Head
10A/10B	Ely (Green Farm Road) to Wood Street
16	Pier Head to Mill Lane via Bute Street

The routes provided a contrasting mix of locations – the drab dockside areas around Pier Head and the picturesque Llandaff Fields and Roath Park. Housing schemes were penetrated at Pengam and Ely, whilst the Gabalfa route ran through Victorian suburbia.

The system now settled down to several years of unchanged operation. By 1961, however, its future came under review, prompted by the need to replace the original 1942 vehicles. The City Council considered the alternative strategies and in October 1961 the decision was taken, like many similar decisions being made around Britain at this time, to replace the trolleybus system with motorbuses.

Despite this pessimism, improvements were made to the operation, particularly to aspects of the overhead equipment. The Transport Department's Chief Engineer, Felix Cunuder, devised a revolutionary automatic frog apparatus, where the whole operation was incorporated into the frog mechanism itself, allowing split second route setting and increased speed under the fittings. His other innovations were the use of space-saving interlaced frogs at two locations on the system, and the design of a lightweight trolley-head to reduce dewirements. These were fitted to all vehicles in the early 1960s.

The run-down of the system was not hurried and did not altogether go as planned. The routes closed as follows, the dates being the last day of trolleybus operation.

Pengam (2/2A)
    24th November 1962
Pier Head via Bute Street (14, ex 16)
    11th January 1964
Victoria Park to City Centre (5/5A/5B)
    24th July 1965
Pier Head to Wood Street (6/9)
    16th December 1965
Llandaff Fields to Wood Street (6)
    16th April 1966
Gabalfa to Wood Street (9)
    16th April 1966
Llandaff Fields to Roath Park (4)
    17thSeptember 1966
Royal Oak to Victoria Park (8)
    17th February 1968
Gabalfa to St Mary Street (1)
    27th April 1968
Roath Park to St Mary Street (3)
    27th April 1968
Ely to Havelock Street (10A/10B)
    3rd December 1969

Services 6 and 9 between Pier Head and Wood Street were abruptly converted to motorbuses following an immediate weight restriction being placed on the Wood Street bridge over the River Taff. There followed a period when trolleybuses on the remaining sections of these routes, from Llandaff Fields and Gabalfa respectively, had to terminate at the Central Bus Station loop and connect with the motorbuses for Pier Head. The Pier Head wiring was, however, left intact for many months, allowing a valedictory enthusiasts' tour to operate over the section (operating empty over the Wood Street bridge) using trolleybus 222 in March 1966.

The final route closure was planned for early 1970. However, the effects of industrial action involving maintenance staff in the previous month led to a severe shortage of serviceable trolleybuses. Because of this, the trolleybuses were withdrawn from service altogether without prior notice after service on 3rd December 1969. However, plans to commemorate the end of trolleybuses were well advanced and allowed to go ahead. Accordingly, during the second week of January 1970, a very limited trolleybus operation was allowed, culminating in a final procession of three trolleybuses from Victoria Park to Roath Depot on the afternoon Sunday 11th January, bringing to an end almost 28 years of operation.

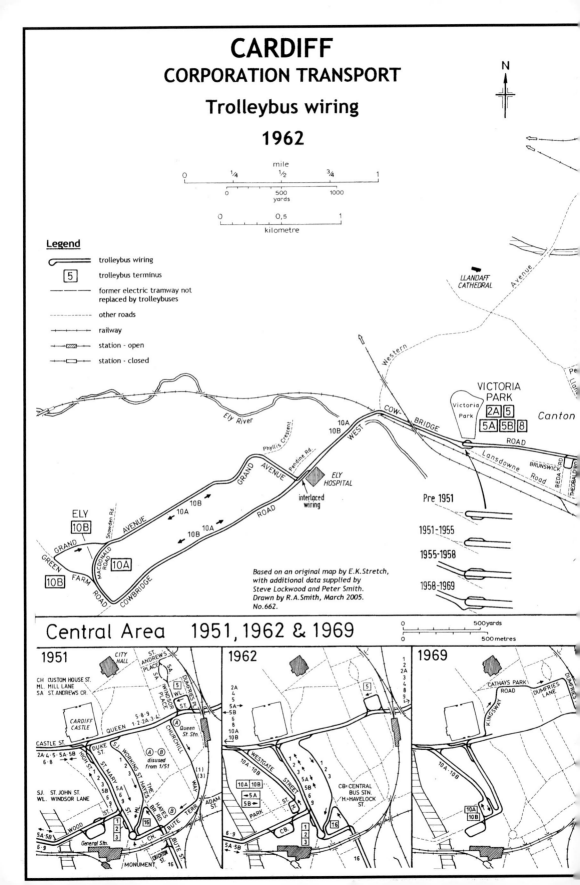

CARDIFF
CORPORATION TRANSPORT
Trolleybus wiring
1962

mile

yards

kilometre

Legend

- trolleybus wiring
- [5] trolleybus terminus
- former electric tramway not replaced by trolleybuses
- other roads
- railway
- station - open
- station - closed

LLANDAFF CATHEDRAL

Western Avenue

Pe Llan

VICTORIA PARK

Victoria Park

Canton

2A [5]
5A 5B 8

Ely River

COW-BRIDGE

WEST ROAD

10A
10B

Phyllis Cresent

Pendine Rd.

Lansdowne Road

BRUNSWICK Road

BEDA RD

THEOBALD

ELY HOSPITAL

interlaced wiring

GRAND AVENUE

Snowden Rd.

AVENUE

10B
10A

10B 10A

ROAD

Pre 1951

1951-1955

1955-1958

1958-1969

ELY
[10B]

GRAND
GREEN FARM ROAD

MACDONALD ROAD

[10A]

[10B]

COWBRIDGE

Based on an original map by E.K.Stretch, with additional data supplied by Steve Lockwood and Peter Smith. Drawn by R.A.Smith, March 2005. No.662.

Central Area   1951, 1962 & 1969

500 yards
500 metres

1951

CITY HALL

ST. ANDREW'S PLACE

CH. CUSTOM HOUSE ST.
ML. MILL LANE
SA. ST ANDREWS CR.

SA
SA
[5]
WINDSOR PLACE
WL
DUMFRIES PL.
ST.

CARDIFF CASTLE

5·8·9
1·2·2A·3·4

QUEEN

(A) Queen St. Stn.

CASTLE ST.

(A)-(B) disused from 1/51

2A·4·5·5A·5B
6·8

HIGH ST.

DUKE ST.

ST. MARY ST.

S. WORKING ST.

CHURCHILL WAY

ST. JOHN ST.

THE HAYES

BUTE BRIDGE RD.

(1)
(3)

ADAM ST.

SJ. ST. JOHN ST.
WL. WINDSOR LANE

WOOD

5A·5B

6·9

General Stn.

CH.

CRICHTON ST.

BUTE ST.

BUTE TERR.

(8)

[16]

[1]
[2]
[3]

MONUMENT

16

1962

1
2
2A
3
4
8
9

2A
4
5
5A
5B
6
8
10A
10B

[5]

WESTGATE STREET

[10A] [10B]
→5A
5B

PARK

1
2
3

1
2
3
5A
5B

CB=CENTRAL BUS STN.
H.=HAVELOCK ST.

[16]

CB

[1]
[2]
[3]

5A·5B

6·9

16

1969

1
2
2A
3
4
8
9
L

CATHAYS PARK
ROAD

DUMFRIES LANE

DUMFRIES

KINGSWAY

10A·10B

10A·10B

10A
10B

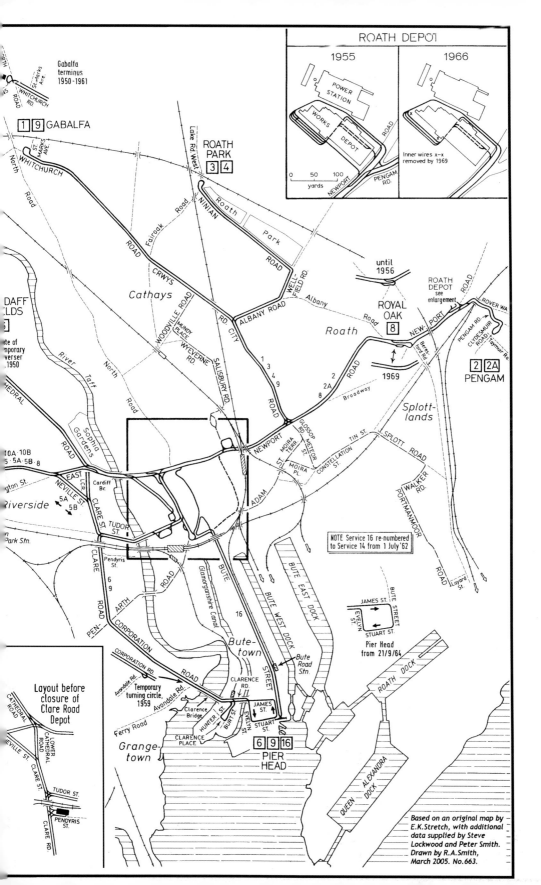

ROATH DEPOT

1955   1966

POWER STATION

WORKS

DEPOT

Inner wires x–x
removed by 1969

0   50   100
yards

NEWPORT   PENGAM RD.

Gabalfa
terminus
1950-1961

St.Marks Ave.

WHITCHURCH RD.

1 9 GABALFA

 St.Marks Ave.

WHITCHURCH

North Road

ROATH
PARK
3 4

Lake Rd. West

Roath   Park

N. NINIAN

Fairoak   Road

Road

CRWYS   ROAD

Cathays

WELLFIELD RD.

until
1956

ROATH
DEPOT
see
enlargement

ROVER WA.

Woodville Road

MUNDY PLACE

WYEVERNE RD.

RD. CITY

SALISBURY RD.

ALBANY ROAD

Albany

Road

ROYAL
OAK
8

NEW-PORT

ROAD

PENGAM RD.

CLYDESMUIR ROAD.

Teymar Rd

DAFF
LDS

te of
mporary
verser
.1950

River   Taff

North   Road

Sophia   Gardens

Roath

1
3
9

ROAD

2
2A
8

Broadway

Berthlwyd Rd.

1969

2 2A
PENGAM

Splott-
lands

HEDRAL

10A · 10B
5 · 5A · 5B · 8

EAST

NEVILLE ST.

LCR

Cardiff Br.

CLARE ST.

TUDOR ST.

NEWPORT

MOIRA TERR.

MOIRA PL.

GLOSSOP RD.

METEOR ST.

CONSTELLATION ST.

TIN ST.

SPLOTT   ROAD

WALKER RD.

PORTMANMOOR   RD.

ROAD

Layard St.

Riverside

5A
5B

6
9

CLARE   ROAD

PEN-

ARTH

CORPORATION   ROAD

Pendyris St.

ADAM

BUTE   STREET

Glamorganshire Canal

Bute-
town

16

NOTE Service 16 re-numbered
to Service 14 from 1 July '62

BUTE   EAST   DOCK

BUTE   WEST   DOCK

JAMES ST.

EVELYN ST.

STUART ST.

BUTE STREET

Pier Head
from 21/9/64

Park Stn.

Layout before
closure of
Clare Road
Depot

CATHEDRAL   ROAD

LOWER CATHEDRAL   ROAD

NEVILLE ST.

CLARE ST.

TUDOR ST.

PENDYRIS ST.

CLARE RD.

CORPORATION RD.

Avondale Rd.

Temporary
turning circle,
1959

Avondale Rd.

Ferry Road

Clarence Bridge

CLARENCE PLACE

CLARENCE RD.

Grange-
town

Bute Road Stn.

HUNTER ST.

BURT ST.

JAMES ST.

EVELYN ST.

STUART ST.

6 9 16
PIER
HEAD

ROATH   DOCK

QUEEN   ALEXANDRA   DOCK

Based on an original map by
E.K.Stretch, with additional
data supplied by Steve
Lockwood and Peter Smith.
Drawn by R.A.Smith,
March 2005. No.663.

CARDIFF
CORPORATION TRANSPORT
Trolleybus
Route Chronology
1942 - 1969

1948

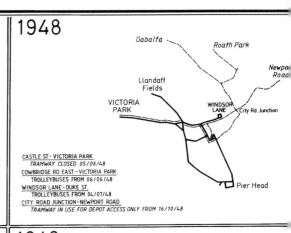

CASTLE ST - VICTORIA PARK
TRAMWAY CLOSED 05/06/48
COWBRIDGE RD EAST - VICTORIA PARK
TROLLEYBUSES FROM 06/06/48
WINDSOR LANE - DUKE ST.
TROLLEYBUSES FROM 04/07/48
CITY ROAD JUNCTION - NEWPORT ROAD
TRAMWAY IN USE FOR DEPOT ACCESS ONLY FROM 16/10/48

1941

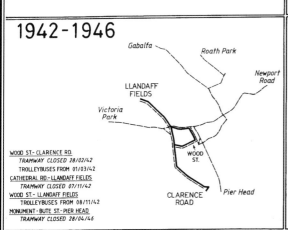

1949

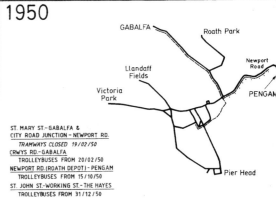

CITY ROAD JUNCTION -
QUEEN ST. - ST MARY ST.
TRAMWAY CLOSED 11/07/49
ALBANY ROAD - ROATH PARK
TRAMWAY CLOSED 02/12/49
QUEEN ST/DUMFRIES PLACE - ROATH PARK
TROLLEYBUSES FROM 03/12/49
CITY ROAD JUNCTION - NEWPORT ROAD
TROLLEYBUSES FROM 03/12/49
(DEPOT ACCESS ONLY UNTIL 15/10/50)
CHURCHILL WAY - BUTE TERRACE
TROLLEYBUSES FROM 03/12/49

1942 - 1946

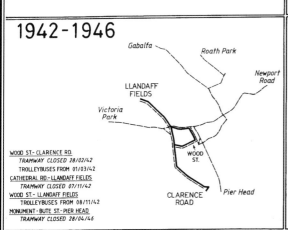

WOOD ST.- CLARENCE RD.
TRAMWAY CLOSED 28/02/42
TROLLEYBUSES FROM 01/03/42
CATHEDRAL RD - LLANDAFF FIELDS
TRAMWAY CLOSED 07/11/42
WOOD ST.- LLANDAFF FIELDS
TROLLEYBUSES FROM 08/11/42
MONUMENT - BUTE ST.- PIER HEAD
TRAMWAY CLOSED 28/04/46

1950

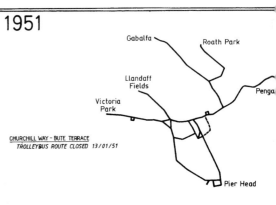

ST. MARY ST.- GABALFA &
CITY ROAD JUNCTION - NEWPORT RD.
TRAMWAYS CLOSED 19/02/50
CRWYS RD.- GABALFA
TROLLEYBUSES FROM 20/02/50
NEWPORT RD.(ROATH DEPOT) - PENGAM
TROLLEYBUSES FROM 15/10/50
ST. JOHN ST.- WORKING ST.- THE HAYES
TROLLEYBUSES FROM 31/12/50

1947

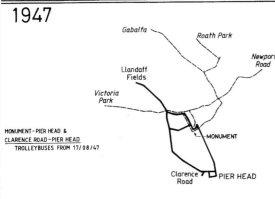

MONUMENT - PIER HEAD &
CLARENCE ROAD - PIER HEAD.
TROLLEYBUSES FROM 17/08/47

1951

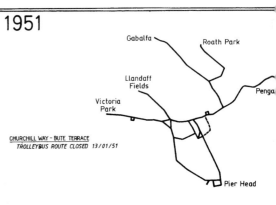

CHURCHILL WAY - BUTE TERRACE
TROLLEYBUS ROUTE CLOSED 13/01/51

S.Lockwood & R.A.Smith 05/2005 Nº 669

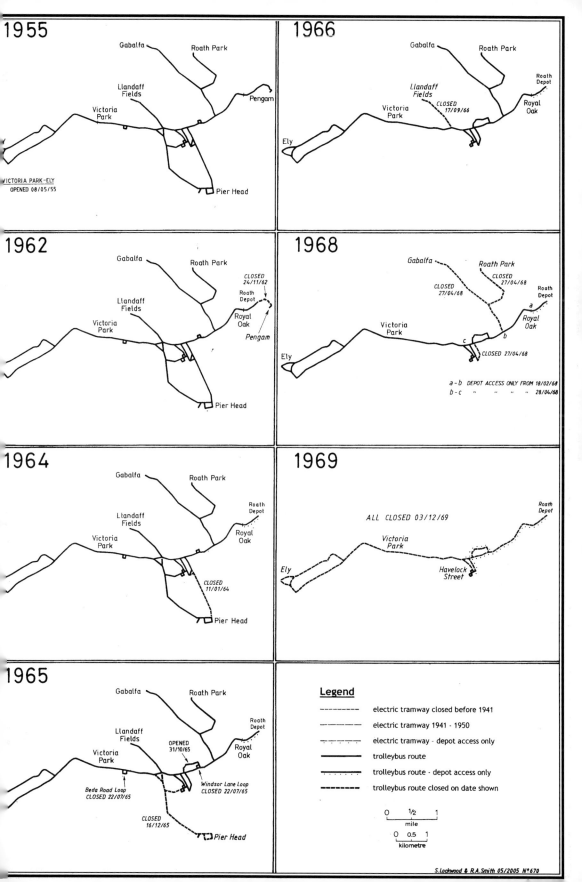

1955

Gabalfa
Roath Park
Llandaff Fields
Pengam
Victoria Park
VICTORIA PARK-ELY
OPENED 08/05/55
Pier Head

1966

Gabalfa
Roath Park
Roath Depot
Llandaff Fields
CLOSED 17/09/66
Victoria Park
Royal Oak
Ely

1962

Gabalfa
Roath Park
CLOSED 24/11/62
Roath Depot
Llandaff Fields
Royal Oak
Victoria Park
Pengam
Pier Head

1968

Gabalfa
Roath Park
CLOSED 27/04/68
CLOSED 27/04/68
Roath Depot
a
Royal Oak
Victoria Park
b
c
CLOSED 27/04/68
Ely
a-b DEPOT ACCESS ONLY FROM 18/02/68
b-c   "   "   "   "   28/04/68

1964

Gabalfa
Roath Park
Roath Depot
Llandaff Fields
Royal Oak
Victoria Park
CLOSED 11/01/64
Pier Head

1969

ALL CLOSED 03/12/69
Roath Depot
Victoria Park
Ely
Havelock Street

1965

Gabalfa
Roath Park
Roath Depot
Llandaff Fields
OPENED 31/10/65
Royal Oak
Victoria Park
Beda Road Loop
CLOSED 22/07/65
Windsor Lane Loop
CLOSED 22/07/65
CLOSED 16/12/65
Pier Head

Legend

– – – – – –	electric tramway closed before 1941
─ · ─ · ─	electric tramway 1941 – 1950
─··─··─	electric tramway – depot access only
──────	trolleybus route
──────	trolleybus route - depot access only
▬ ▬ ▬ ▬	trolleybus route closed on date shown

0   ½   1
mile

0   0.5   1
kilometre

S.Lockwood & R.A.Smith 05/2005 Nº670

TRAMS TO TROLLEYBUSES

1.   Almost from the start of operations the trolleybuses ran along Castle Street beside Cardiff Castle. This 1947 scene, in the year that the Castle was given to the city by the Marquis of Bute, shows AEC trolleybus 206, still in wartime grey livery and out-numbered by trams. It is working on the only trolleybus route in operation at that time. Both 206, and tram 102 beside it, will turn right into High Street using their own separate overhead wires. The tram is on the Victoria Park service and will terminate in the city centre, at Bute Terrace whilst 206 will continue beyond the centre to Clarence Road. (IL Wright)

2. The next route to be converted to trolleybuses was a short shuttle from the Pier Head to the city centre via Bute Street. This occurred in August 1947, following a period of 16 months when motorbuses temporarily replaced the trams. Seven elderly second-hand single–deck trolleybuses from Pontypridd, were used. This view shows trolleybus 236 near the Monument terminus of the service on 8th April 1948. Tram 4 on the left is on the Victoria Park service which would be converted to trolleybuses in the following June. Note the "pay as you enter" (PAYE) sign in the tram's windscreen. (CW Routh collection)

3. The tram routes on the east side of the city began to be replaced by trolleybuses from early December 1949 when the Roath Park service was converted. This is a scene in City Road during the eleven week period when the Roath Park trolleybuses ran alongside the Whitchurch Road trams, the last in the city. Tram 92 is being crowded out by new trolleybuses 256 (left) and 246 on 15th February 1950. (IL Wright)

4.   Trolleybus overhead is being erected in this view of Whitchurch Road tram terminus on 12th February 1950. The trolleybuses ran beyond this point to turn round outside the Regal Dance Hall at far side of the junction with North Road (see photograph 10). The leading tower wagon in this scene was formerly a 1936 Leyland TD4c bus which had been only recently converted into its new guise. (IL Wright)

5.　　Cardiff's last normal service tram ran to Whitchurch Road on 19th February 1950. The following day trolleybuses took over and tram 11, elaborately decorated, ran on the route carrying the public prior to a formal civic closure ceremony. It is seen here emerging from Custom House Street, near the Monument, accompanied by trolleybus 249. This is a very rare view of a double-deck trolleybus in Custom House Street, whilst using the one-way routeing from Queen Street via Churchill Way. This was only in operation between December 1949 and January 1951. (IL Wright)

6.　　To achieve the replacement of the trams, Cardiff purchased fifty BUT double-deck trolleybuses bodied to its own specification in partnership with East Lancashire Coachbuilders. In the summer of 1948, trolleybus 229 is seen in Wolverhampton whilst being towed from the coachbuilder's factory at Blackburn to Cardiff.
(RF Mack collection/Trolleybus Museum Company)

PAY AS YOU ENTER

7.   The inauguration of trolleybuses in 1942 coincided with the introduction of the flat-fare (1d) "pay as you enter" (PAYE) system of fare collection. This view, taken after the war, shows grey liveried AEC trolleybus 207 loading passengers in Wood Street, with the prominent PAYE signs in the nearside lower deck windows. (English Electric/C Taylor collection)

8.   This less than perfect view of new single-deck BUT trolleybus 242 at Pier Head also shows the PAYE signs beside the entrance. Of especial interest in this view are the black-on-white destination blinds, a feature that was not perpetuated. (RF Mack collection/Trolleybus Museum Company)

9.   The BUT double-deckers were designed specially for PAYE operation and incorporated a conductor's seat, visible here on trolleybus 268 alongside the rear bulkhead beside the platform. This vehicle was one of those whose bodywork was built in Cardiff by Bruce Coachworks, and the oval bodybuilders' plate can be seen below the conductor's seat. (The Omnibus Society collection)

CARDIFF CORPORATION
TRANSPORT DEPARTMENT
Instructions to Conductors in charge of Trolleybuses

For the assistance and guidance of conductors in charge of Trolleybuses, the following main points are outlined and must be strictly observed :-

1   The conductor will take up his position on the platform at the entrance to the lower saloon with a clear view of all passengers boarding, in order to ensure that both lower and upper deck passengers deposit their pennies in the 'pay as you enter' box.

2   No change will be given. No names and addresses will be taken, and postage stamps will not be accepted in lieu of fares. Passengers boarding the vehicle with luggage which would normally be charged for, will deposit such charge of twopence in the 'pay as you enter' box. It will be in order to permit one passenger to place a silver coin in the box, say a sixpenny piece, to cover the travel of six passengers, but on no account must a conductor accept any money from passengers.

3   Every conductor will be issued each day with an emergency ticket box, to be used only in the event of the 'pay as you enter' box becoming jambed. (sic) Immediately following any jambing of the cash machine, the conductor should telephone Clare Road depot in order that the defect may be remedied.

4   Conductors must not under any circumstances enter into argument with passengers as to whether the fare has been paid, but should make report at once to office as to the incident, for purposes of record.

5   Conductors will be provided with a ticket nipper for use when prepaid tickets are presented. These prepaid tickets will be dealt with by the conductor in the usual way.

6   Upon the arrival of a Trolleybus at a terminal point, conductors will ensure that all passengers alight from the vehicle. At such terminal point the rear platform must throughout the whole period of 'stand' time be under the constant supervision of either the conductor or the driver. It will be clear that in the absence of the conductor and driver from the rear platform at a terminal point any number of passengers could enter the vehicle without payment of fare.

7   Conductors will be supplied with special vehicle waybills, and the method of completion will be explained on special notices posted in the depots.

Special Note: There is no restriction as to the number of passengers allowed to stand in the Trolleybus - but no passengers shall be allowed to stand on the upper deck.

Central Offices
John W Dunning
Womanby Street, Cardiff.
Traffic Manager
18th February, 1942.

GABALFA

10.   The No. 1 Gabalfa trolleybus service opened in February 1950, replacing the Whitchurch Road trams. Difficulties in finding a suitable turning space resulted in a turning circle being constructed at the far side of the Whitchurch Road/North Road junction outside the Regal Dance Hall. BUT 271 is shown at the terminus in the early 1950s. The front exit door, later removed, is prominent in this view.(R Marshall)

11.   Another view of the original Gabalfa trolleybus terminus is seen here showing AEC 203 waiting to return to St Mary Street. (J White)

12.   Increased road traffic resulted in the Transport Department reviewing the terminal provision at Gabalfa. The result was that from May 1961 a new turning arrangement was brought into use on the south side of the Whitchurch Road/North Road junction. A private road was created near the junction with St Mark's Avenue, which involved the demolition of some housing. The new terminus is seen here in July 1963, showing trolleybuses 253 and 254. The truncated house end behind the trolleybus can be seen. Also of note is the sign on the traction pole to the right of 253 indicating the private road for trolleybuses only. Service 9 was an additional trolleybus service to Gabalfa which was introduced in October 1951 giving a direct link through the city centre to Clarence Road and Pier Head. (CW Routh)

13.   This is Whitchurch Road near the former tram terminus, showing trolleybus 252 which has just turned out of the terminal loop at the start of its journey to St Mary Street. A corporation motorbus passes by in the opposite direction. (RF Mack/Trolleybus Museum Company)

14. Further south, beyond Cathays Cemetery, Whitchurch Road becomes Crwys Road. Just north of the junction with Albany Road, where the Roath Park route branched off from the Gabalfa service, Crwys Road crosses the former Rhymney Railway line from Queen Street Station to Caerphilly and beyond. In this view, trolleybus 213 is crossing the bridge over the line. (RF Mack/Trolleybus Museum Company)

Trolley Bus Service No. 3

Service No. 3.—ROATH PARK and ST. MARY STREET.
INWARD to City Centre via Newport Rd., Queen St., Churchill Way, Bute Terr., and Custom House St. to St. Mary St. OUTWARD via St. Mary St., High St., Duke St. and Queen St., etc.

From Roath Park to St. Mary Street.		From St. Mary Street to Roath Park.	
Monday to Saturday.	Sunday.	Monday to Saturday.	Sunday.
a.m.	a.m.	a.m.	a.m.
5– 0, 20, 40	———	5–17, 37, 57	———
6– 0, 20, 40	———	6–17, 37, 57	———
7– 0, 10, 20, 30, 40, 50	———	7–17, 27, 37, 47, 57	7–50
8– 0, 5, 10, 15, 19, 24, 29, 34, 38, 43, 48, 53, 57	8–10	8– 7, 17, 22, 27, 32, 36, 41, 46, 51, 55	8–49
9– 2, 7, 12, 16, 22 and every 6 or 7 mins. until	9–12, 32, 52 and every 20 mins. until	9– 0, 5, 14, 19, 24, 33 and every 6 or 7 mins. until	9–29, 49 and every 20 mins. until
p.m.	p.m.	p.m.	p.m.
12–26, 31, 36, 41, 45, 50, 55	12–52	12–24, 27, 30, 36, 43, 48 53, 58	12– 9, 29, 49
1– 0, 4, 9, 14, 19, 23, 28, 33, 38, 42, 47, 52, 57	1–12, 27, 32, 48, 55	1– 2, 7, 12, 17, 21, 26, 31, 36, 40, 45, 50, 55, 59	1– 9, 29, 39, 44, 49, 59
2– 1, 6 and every 4 or 5 mins. until	2– 1, 7 and every 6 or 7 mins. until	2– 4, 9 and every 4 or 5 mins. until	2– 7, 12 and every 6 or 7 mins. until
5–40, 45, 49, 54, 59	9–31, 37, 43, 50, 56	5–38, 43, 47, 52, 57	
6– 6, 13, 19 and every 6 or 7 mins. until		6– 2, 6, 11, 16 & every 6 or 7 mins. until	
10– 1, 7, 13, 20, 26, 32, 39, 45, 51	10– 2, 9, 15, 22, 28, 40	10– 5, 11, 18, 24, 30, 37, 45	10– 0, 7, 13, 19, 26, 32, 39, 45

ROATH PARK

15.   The Roath Park trolleybus route served one of the main recreational parks for Cardiff's citizens. As with the Gabalfa service, two routes served Roath Park, service 3 to St Mary Street and service 4 via the city centre to Llandaff Fields. Two trolleybuses are shown here at the alighting stop in Ninian Road at the terminus with the park in the background. (DG Bowen/C Taylor)

16.   Trolleybuses turned using the roundabout at the junction of Ninian Road and Fairoak Road. This was on the site of the tram turning loop. AEC trolleybus 202, with attachments on its sides for Christmas illuminations, is seen starting the turn. (DG Bowen/C Taylor)

17.   Trolleybus 262 turns back onto Ninian Road to reach the terminal stop. Note the former tram terminus passenger shelter in the right background. (DG Bowen/C Taylor)

18.   Leaving the terminus, trolleybuses ran along the length of Ninian Road which skirted Roath Park itself. At Pen-y-Lan Road junction the route turned into Wellfield Road where trolleybus 215 is seen negotiating the turn, with Ninian Road and the park in the background. (DG Bowen/C Taylor)

19.   After a short run along Wellfield Road, the route turned right into suburban Albany Road. At the western end of Albany Road is City Road junction, where the Gabalfa route was joined. Here trolleybus 285 is seen pulling away from the traffic lights before turning left into City Road. (DG Bowen/C Taylor)

20.   The Roath Park and Gabalfa routes diverged at the junction of Albany Road, Crwys Road and City Road. This view, taken from City Road, shows trolleybus 221 proceeding across the junction from Crwys Road on its way to St Mary Street. The Roath Park route turns right here into Albany Road. (J White)

21.   At the Newport Road end of City Road, the Gabalfa and Roath Park routes turned right towards the city centre, although the wiring junction here included connections to turn in the opposite direction for depot journeys. Trolleybus 219, outbound to Roath Park turns from Newport Road into City Road in this 1966 view. (RF Mack / Trolleybus Museum Company)

22.   Turning from City Road into Newport Road is AEC 209, bound for Llandaff Fields. This view was taken during the period of changeover from the standard trolley-head to Cardiff's own lightweight design. The AEC has the older type heads whereas the following BUT vehicle sports the new, much smaller, type. (J White)

23. This is trolleybus 213 running from Roath Depot, turning into City Road to take up service. (DG Bowen/C Taylor)

PENGAM AND NEWPORT ROAD

24. The last former tram service to become trolleybus operated was that to Newport Road, where Roath Depot was situated at the tram terminus. However, the trolleybuses were extended a short distance into the Pengam housing scheme, where they turned by means of an elongated island at Clydesmuir Road. Typically, two services served Pengam, route 2 to St Mary Street and a peak hours service 2A which ran to Victoria Park. This route was the first to be abandoned in November 1962, although only the short section of overhead between the terminus and the depot became disused. The terminus was very close to Pengam Airport, where the Bruce-bodied trolleybuses were constructed and appropriately enough this view shows two of these, 254 and 256, at the terminus shortly before the route ended. No. 254 on the left is operating the 2A service to Victoria Park. (DG Bowen/C Taylor)

25.　　Between Pengam terminus and Roath Depot, the route crossed the former GWR main railway line. Unusually, access to the depot from Pengam was by a crossover wire onto the outbound overhead wires. This view shows 1955 BUT 279, having crossed the railway and approaching the crossover. (DG Bowen/C Taylor)

26.　　Looking in the opposite direction from the previous photograph, trolleybus 253 climbs onto the railway bridge from Newport Road en route for Pengam. The electricity power station adjacent to Roath Depot dominates the background.　　(DG Bowen/C Taylor)

27.　Following the demise of the Pengam route, the wiring between Roath Depot and the Royal Oak was retained for depot access purposes. This stretch included a railway bridge carrying the docks branch over Newport Road. Strict speed restrictions applied when trolleybuses were passing under such bridges and if the driver got it wrong this was the result. In July 1963, 1955 BUT 287, the highest numbered vehicle in the fleet, has dewired whilst operating from the depot to the city centre to take up service on route 10A. (JS King)

28.　At the Newport Road and Broadway junction, a turning point was provided at the roundabout. This was designated 'Royal Oak' after the hostelry at this location. Trolleybus service 8 terminated here, running through the city centre to Victoria Park. The service lasted until February 1968 and the turn-back wiring was removed some months afterwards when road improvements resulted in the removal of the roundabout. This view dated August 1965 shows trolleybus 215 negotiating the turning loop followed by sister vehicle 220. (RD Hellyar-Symons)

Trolley Bus Service No. 2

Service No. 2.—ST. MARY STREET and PENGAM

From ST. MARY STREET.

MONDAYS to SATURDAYS.	SUNDAYS.
a.m. **5**—15, 30, 32V, 48 **6**—0, 2V, 14V, 15, 26V, 27, 38V, 39, 50V, 51 **7**—2V, 3, 14V, 15, 26V, 27, 38V, 39, 51 53V, 59 **8**—5, 11, 17, 23, 29, 35, 41, 47, 53, 59 **9**—5, 11, 17, 23, 29, 35, 41, 47, 53, 59	**a.m.** **5**—25V **6**—23V, 36V **7**—30 **8**—6, 42 **9**—18, 54 **10**—12, 30, 48 **11**—6, 24, 42
and at similar intervals, i.e., every 6 minutes until	**p.m.** **12**—0, 18, 36, 54 **1**—12, 30, 48, 53R **2**—OR, 6, 11R, 18R, 24, 29R, 36R, 42, 47R, 54R
p.m. **9**—5, 11, 17, 23, 29, 35, 41, 47, 53, 59 **10**—5, 11, 17, 23, 29, 35, 41, 47	**3**—0, 5R, 12R, 18, 23R, 30R, 36, 41R, 48R, 54, 59R **4**—6R, 12, 17R, 24R, 30, 35R, 42R, 48, 53R
Note.—Additional journeys will be operated between St. Mary St. and New- port Rd. Royal Oak, to augment the above service during the following periods :— 8.0 a.m. until 9. 0 a.m. Mondays to Saturdays. 12.30 p.m. until 2.30 p.m. Mondays to Fridays. 4.30 p.m. until 6.30 p.m. Mondays to Fridays. 12-0 noon until 10.44 p.m. Saturdays.	**5**—OR, 6, 11R, 18R, 24, 29R, 36R, 42, 47R, 54R **6**—0, 5R, 12R, 18, 23R, 30R, 36, 41R, 48R, 54, 59R **7**—6R, 12, 17R, 24R, 30, 35R, 42R, 48, 53R **8**—OR, 6, 11R, 18R, 24, 29R, 36R, 42, 47R, 54R **9**—0, 5R, 12R, 18, 23R, 30R, 36, 41R, 48R, 54, 59R **10**—6R, 12, 17R, 23R, 30R, 36R, 42R, 48.

29. A passing loop in the overhead wiring was provided to allow trolleybuses proceeding from the depot to pass a vehicle standing at the Royal Oak terminus. This situation is depicted here showing trolleybus 216 running from the depot passing 273 in the terminal loop. Note that both vehicles have had their original front destination glasses replaced by more modern rubber mounted fittings.
(DG Bowen/C Taylor)

30. Near the city centre, trolleybus 215 is seen in Newport Road approaching the City Road junction en-route to Royal Oak in 1967. Note the subtle difference in livery style with the one carried by this same vehicle in 1965 shown in photograph 27. The Guy motorbus on the left is operating on the former tram service between Clive Street, Grangetown and Splott, which was operated by single-deck bogie trams until converted to motorbuses in 1936. (CW Routh)

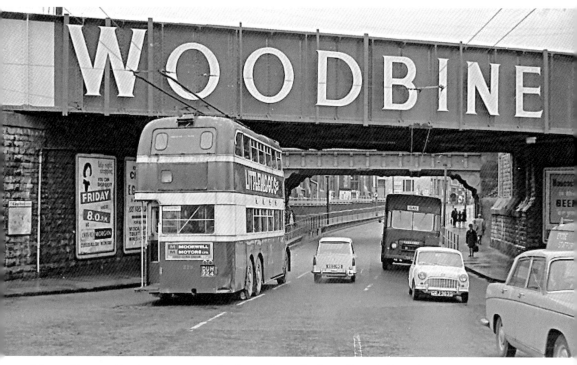

31.   Newport Road commences at the Queen Street Station railway bridges, beyond which is Queen Street in the city centre. The road under these bridges needed to be lowered to allow trolleybus operation. Trolleybus 229 is about to dip under the bridges. (RF Mack/Trolleybus Museum Company)

PIER HEAD AND BUTE STREET

32.   Probably the best remembered Cardiff trolleybus service is the Pier Head via Bute Street route that operated with single-deck vehicles. The service terminated literally at the waters' edge at Pier Head, from where pleasure steamers crossed the Bristol Channel to Weston-Super-Mare and Ilfracombe. The area served by the route was the legendary Tiger Bay, with its proliferation of warehouses and public houses. Trolleybuses turned by way of a reversing triangle, the only such example in regular use in Cardiff. Seen in this view is one of the 1949 BUT single-deckers which replaced the second-hand ex-Pontypridd vehicles. Trolleybus 242 is at the end of the wires in Stuart Street prior to reversing. (C Carter)

→

33.   Looking in the opposite direction from the previous photograph, trolleybus 241 is about to reverse. Note that, against regulations, the conductor is looking out of the rear window of the vehicle rather than supervising the reverse from outside. The set of wires to the right of the vehicle was part of the turning loop of the Pier Head via Clarence Road service, which also terminated at this point. (RK Blencowe)

→

34.   This view shows 243, the sole additional single-deck trolleybus, which entered service in 1955. It is in the process of reversing, guided by the conductor. Emerging from Stuart Street is a trolleybus on the Clarence Road service which will turn left to reach its terminal stop. (DG Bowen/C Taylor)

35.   One of the original ex-Pontypridd English Electric trolleybuses is seen having reversed, and ready to turn right to reach the terminal loading stop. It is painted in the grey livery that most of this batch of vehicles spent their short life in Cardiff. They were nicknamed 'Doodlebugs' because of their distinctive noise and low speed. This name was used to describe trolleybuses on the Bute Street route even after the withdrawal of the ex Pontypridd vehicles. (S Lockwood collection)

36.   Both the Pier Head trolleybus services shared adjacent loading stands. Trolleybus 241 is seen loading passengers, with a vehicle on the Clarence Road service in front. The double-decker will turn left into James Street shortly after leaving the stop. This view dates from January 1952. (Photoarchives)

Dont's for Trolleybus Conductors

DON'T

Forget when putting the trolleys to the wires, to put the 'Negative' up first

Forget when taking the trolleys away from the wires to take the 'Negative' away last

Forget that 'Negative' is always the left hand or near-side wire of each pair.

Forget the instructions you received in the matter of dealing with electrical leakages on trolleybuses.

Be afraid to ask for further instruction if you are still uncertain as to what you should do under such circumstances.

Fail to give definite signals to the driver when he is reversing the trolleybus.

Forget that you must stand in the roadway to give such signal, and use the whistle.

Fail to observe, when operating switch frogs, that (a) your own trolleys have taken the correct wires, and (b) that the frogs go back to their proper positions upon release.

Forget that the Trolleybus, the revenue and the passengers, are entrusted to your care for safe keeping and safe conduct.

Be offensive when exercising authority and control over the passengers.

Forget that intending passengers have every right to know where YOUR Trolleybus is going.

37.   Approaching the terminus in August 1957 after the run along Bute Street is trolleybus 238, the first of the 1949 single-deckers. This was where the trams reversed. The exit wiring from the reverser can be seen. For most of its life the Bute Street service was numbered 16, being re-numbered to 14 in July 1962, some nineteen months before the route was converted to motorbuses. (IL Wright)

← ————— 38. At the city centre end of Bute Street, the route was crossed by the former Great Western main line railway on its approach to Cardiff General Station. The bridge was the lowest encountered on the system, hence the necessity for single-deck operation. In tram days, the special low height design of the later cars allowed double-deck trams on the route. Even though Cardiff's own design of trolleybus was of low height, this bridge's headroom was still too low. In 1950, a reverser was constructed at Crichton Street on the Pier Head side of the bridge to allow the vehicles to turn whilst major road reconstruction was taking place in Custom House Street. The reverser was also useful when the roadway under the bridge became flooded, which was a regular occurrence. Despite this, the facility was removed later in the 1950s. Trolleybus 240 is seen emerging from under the bridge en route for Pier Head. Crichton Street is situated behind the camera. (R Marshall)

(lower left) 39. Trolleybus 241 is seen at the traffic lights at the city centre side of the bridge, ready to cross into Hayes Bridge Road. Note that double-deck motorbuses were able to negotiate the bridge as seen here. (RF Mack / Trolleybus Museum Company)

PIER HEAD
AND
CLARENCE ROAD

40. We return to Pier Head Terminus to look at the other route to this point, which was via Clarence Road and Clarence Bridge. Two services used the route, no. 6 to Llandaff Fields and no 9. to Gabalfa. The turning arrangement for these services was a one-way loop via Evelyn Street, Stuart Street, Bute Street and James Street, but in 1964, after the abandonment of the single-deck service, the loop was reversed in direction. Trolleybus 269 is seen at the terminal stop together with Bute Street single-decker 240. (M Rooum)

41.   At the western end of James Street, the route crossed the Glamorganshire Canal at the James Street swing bridge. Special electrical connections had to be provided in the trolleybus overhead at this point when the route was extended in August 1947, but this necessity was short lived as the bridge ceased to be operational in 1948. Running alongside the canal on the west side was the Glamorganshire Canal Railway, which served industries along the western bank. Both canal and railway were owned by Cardiff Corporation since 1944, the canal closing in 1951. However, the railway lasted until 1963, and was latterly worked by a Greenwood and Batley battery locomotive. This scene shows the locomotive with a single wagon passing under the trolleybus overhead with the swing bridge in the background on 2nd August 1957, just before the bridge was dismantled. On the extreme left is the control tower from where the bridge was formerly operated. The locomotive, known as 'Greenbat', was painted in the same crimson-lake livery of the trolleybuses complete with the city coat-of-arms. (IL Wright)

42. The Clarence Road route was Cardiff's first trolleybus route and the original terminus between 1942 and 1947, was just beyond Clarence Bridge at Hunter Street, opposite Clarence Road Station as shown here. The vehicles turned by way of a 'round the houses' loop via Burt Street, Clarence Place and Hunter Street. From 1947 the route was extended to Pier Head, although the original loop was left in situ for short workings until the end of the route in December 1965. In the early 1950s, trolleybus 218 is seen turning into the loop before operating back to Gabalfa. (RK Blencowe)

43. Between April and June 1964, sewer works prevented the operation of trolleybuses to Pier Head, and the service terminated at the Hunter Street loop. This is Burt Street showing trolleybus 263 and also the wiring turning into Clarence Place. (DG Bowen/C Taylor)

44.   One of the sights of the Cardiff trolleybus system was the Clarence Bridge over the River Taff connecting the Grangetown area with the docks at the end of Corporation Road. The lattice girder bridge was built in 1890 and had previously carried trams. A strict 5 mph speed limit applied to trolleybuses whist crossing the structure. Seen completing the crossing of the bridge from Grangetown is trolleybus 229 on service 6 from Llandaff Fields. During the course of the journey it will have crossed the River Taff three times; at Cardiff Bridge, Wood Street Bridge and then here. (DG Bowen/C Taylor)

→

45.   At the northern end of Corporation Road was the junction with Penarth Road in Grangetown. Trolleybus 246 is seen in Clare Road waiting to cross into Corporation Road.
(C Carter)

→

46.   Crossing Clare Road is another railway bridge carrying the Great Western main line west from Cardiff General Station. Cardiff's first trolleybus depot was situated at the Pier Head side of the bridge, until 1953 (see photograph 102). This later view shows trolleybus 218 proceeding towards Pier Head. The depot was on the right out of view. Note that the vehicle still has the front exit in situ.
(DA Jones / London Trolleybus Preservation Society).

47. Being on Cardiff's first trolleybus route, it is appropriate to include this 1946 view of one of the original trolleybus fleet, AEC 203 passing under the Clare Road bridge. Note the vehicle's wartime grey livery with white marker paint. (English Electric / C Taylor collection)

48. Another view of the Clare Road bridge, shows the Tudor Street junction in the background. Here services 6 and 9 turned right into Tudor Street to travel via Wood Street to the city centre. There were also wiring connections from Tudor Street into Clare Street for the service 5A and 5B routes to and from Victoria Park via Neville Street. Trolleybus 250 is under the bridge and another can be seen ready to turn right into Tudor Street. (C.Carter)

49.   This is a view of Neville Street at the junction with Clare Street showing trolleybus 259 operating on service 5B from Victoria Park. The wiring in the upper foreground proceeds into Lower Cathedral Road and is the former depot link from Clare Road depot leading directly to Cathedral Road. The crossing at Cowbridge Road was removed when the depot closed, but the remainder of the wiring along Lower Cathedral Road was retained to allow it to be used as a diversionary route for the Llandaff Fields service (see photograph 55). (DG Bowen/C Taylor)

LLANDAFF FIELDS

50.   Probably the most picturesque Cardiff trolleybus terminus was at Llandaff Fields. It was served by two routes, service 4 to Roath Park and service 6 to Pier Head. Vehicles turned by way of a private turning circle at the entrance to the Fields on the site of the tram stub terminus. This had been Cardiff's last tramway extension in 1928, and the only example in the city of reserved track. Seen here is trolleybus 219 about to turn on the circle with 230 in the background at the terminal stop.
(CW Routh)

51.   Trolleybus 271 is seen mid-way round the circle showing the pleasant aspect of the terminus. (RF Mack / Trolleybus Museum Company)

52.   This 1950s view shows two trolleybuses, 256 and 273, at the terminal stop. Note the full blind display on the rear of these vehicles. These were reduced to show only a service number in the early 1960s. (RFMack / Trolleybus Museum Company)

53.   Llandaff Fields was reached from Cowbridge Road via Cathedral Road. Even in the rain, as shown here, this is an extremely pleasant tree-lined residential street. Trolleybus 229 is seen near the Cowbridge Road junction, proceeding towards the terminus. (RF Mack / Trolleybus Museum Company)

54.   Prior to the closure of Clare Road Depot in 1953, the wiring at the Cathedral Road / Cowbridge Road junction allowed vehicles to cross to and from Lower Cathedral Road for depot workings. These junctions were removed in 1953, but the Lower Cathedral Road wiring was retained for emergency use until the mid-1960s. One such occasion was the annual Miners Gala, when some main streets in the city centre were closed. Cathedral Road trolleybuses then had to cross Cowbridge Road using traction batteries to reach the wires at the other side to resume their journeys, diverting via Wood Street. This view shows trolleybus 223 in the process of crossing Cowbridge Road into Lower Cathedral Road. (DG Bowen/C Taylor)

55. This is the scene on a similar occasion as the previous photograph, taken further along Lower Cathedral Road near the junction with Neville Street. Trolleybus 255 has travelled from the city centre via Wood Street and Tudor Street and will cross Cowbridge Road on battery power to regain its normal route. On the right, 1955 BUT trolleybus is emerging from Neville Street probably on a diverted Ely service working and it will run into the city centre via Wood Street. (DG Bowen/C Taylor)

ELY
AND
VICTORIA PARK

56. The final development of the Cardiff trolleybus system was the four miles of wiring extending the Cowbridge Road service westwards beyond Victoria Park into the Ely housing scheme. This came into use in May 1955. The extension took the form of an elongated loop, worked in both directions, service 10A operating anti-clockwise and service 10B clockwise. The route diverged at Ely Hospital near Pendine Road, as seen here, showing trolleybus 277 on a 10B working. The 10A wires turn right into Grand Avenue. Note the interlaced wiring at this junction and the re-built upper deck front of the vehicle, the only one of the 1955 batch to be so treated. (DG Bowen/C Taylor)

57.　　Service 10B turned into the housing area at Green Farm Road, which climbed steeply away from Cowbridge Road. AEC trolleybus 201 is seen turning back onto Cowbridge Road on service 10A. Note the Christmas illuminations on the vehicle. (DG Bowen/C Taylor)

58.　　The main service operated between Green Farm Road and Grand Avenue via McDonald Road. However, a limited number of service 10B workings were diverted via a one-way loop, continuing along Green Farm Road to its junction with Grand Avenue. This served the western edge of the housing and Cardiff's Western Cemetery. Trolleybus 255, complete with Christmas illuminations, has climbed the hill from Cowbridge Road and is seen turning onto the diversion. The vehicles did not carry any separate indication to signify if the alternative 10B routing was being taken. (DG Bowen/C Taylor)

59.   Trolleybus 283 is seen at the Green Farm Road (Western Cemetery) terminus before turning into Grand Avenue to resume its journey back to the city centre. Approximately one in three 10B journeys were diverted to here, this being the most westerly point of the system.
(RF Mack / Trolleybus Museum Company)

60.   The 10A, and the main 10B services, both had their terminal stops in McDonald Road. Here, trolleybus 227 is seen on service 10A, with the rear of 275 in view on service 10B.
(RF Mack / Trolleybus Museum Company)

61.   The main road through the housing area is Grand Avenue. In the 1920s, it was proposed to extend the Victoria Park tram route along here, using the central grass strip as a reservation. This did not come to fruition. The width of the road meant that bracket arm wiring suspension was used for the trolleybuses. Trolleybus 277 is seen proceeding towards McDonald Road on service 10A.
(RF Mack / Trolleybus Museum Company)

62.   At Phyllis Crescent, Grand Avenue turns and descends to the junction with Cowbridge Road. This interesting scene at Phyllis Crescent during roadworks, shows trolleybus 283 on service 10A, operating 'single line' on the wrong side of Grand Avenue. (DG Bowen/C Taylor))

63.   Having re-joined Cowbridge Road West, the route crossed the Ely River. In April 1969, the structure of the bridge was found to be unsafe, and temporary 'Bailey' bridges were provided to maintain the busy traffic flow, causing considerable adjustments to the overhead wiring. Trolleybus 281 is seen on an inbound journey from Ely negotiating the bridge. (DG Bowen/C Taylor)

64.   At the Western Avenue roundabout, Cowbridge Road West became Cowbridge Road East. Also at this point, the Great Western main line railway passed under the road. Trolleybus 218 negotiates the roundabout with Western Avenue on the right.
(RF Mack / Trolleybus Museum Company)

65.   Between Western Avenue and Victoria Park, the Radyr branch railway crossed over Cowbridge Road East. Trolleybus 275 passes under the bridge en route from Ely to the city centre.
(RF Mack / Trolleybus Museum Company)

66.	Victoria Park was a major point on the trolleybus system. Several services terminated here, some of which operated at peak hours only, and from 1955 it was an intermediate point on the Ely route. This view, however, shows the terminal stop before 1955 when Victoria Park was the limit of operations. Trolleybus 221 is on service 5B, which ran as a circular service to Wood Street via Neville Street, returning to Victoria Park via Castle Street and Cardiff Bridge. Service 5A ran in the opposite direction and in later years they operated at peak hours only.
(Ipswich Transport Museum collection)

67.	The wiring arrangements for trolleybuses turning at Victoria Park varied over the years, and a major feature of the layout was that the turn across Cowbridge Road East was at a traffic roundabout and against the traffic flow. The excellent sight lines meant this arrangement operated without any problems. Trolleybus 273, turning-round on service 8, demonstrates the procedure in the face of on-coming traffic. (DG Bowen/C Taylor)

68.	The terminal stand included a loop to allow trolleybuses to pass. Trolleybus 253 on the left working service 10A is overtaking 256 waiting to start a journey on service 8 to Royal Oak. Compare the upper–deck fronts of the two vehicles, 256 in rebuilt form and 253 in original condition.
(RF Mack / Trolleybus Museum Company)

←————— 69.	Cowbridge Road East between Victoria Park and Cardiff Bridge was in the Canton district of Cardiff and parts of it were quite narrow for such a main road. Two Ely service trolleybuses pass each other in this section, 218 on the left and 283 on the right. (RF Mack / Trolleybus Museum Company)

(lower left) 70.	Service 5B diverged from Cowbridge Road East to run via Neville Street and Wood Street into the city centre. The junction was outside St David's Hospital, on the right in this view, and trolleybus 262 is seen turning into Neville Street. It will return to Victoria Park via St Mary Street and Cardiff Bridge. Service 5A operated in the opposite direction. Withdrawn from service in 1968, this vehicle was preserved and had its panelled over front exit door re-instated, becoming Cardiff's last trolleybus to operate in January 1970.	(DG Bowen / C Taylor)

WINDSOR LANE AND
CATHAYS PARK ROAD

71.	Trolleybuses from the Newport Road direction ran into the city centre via Queen Street, having first passed under the Queen Street railway bridges. A turn-round facility was provided at the east end of Queen Street by means of a 'round-the-houses' loop via Dumfries Place, Windsor Lane and Windsor Place. This could be used from either the Newport Road or city centre directions. It was the terminal point for service 5 from Victoria Park and also some peak-hour extras on services 1 and 3. It was also useful when the city centre streets were closed for special events. The loop was removed when service 5 was withdrawn in July 1965. This view shows trolleybus 228 turning into Dumfries Place on a terminating service from the Newport Road direction. (DG Bowen / C Taylor)

72.   BUT 228 is seen again, this time working on service 5. It has just departed from the terminal stop in Windsor Lane and is negotiating the turn into Windsor Place en route for Victoria Park.
(CW Routh)

Trolley Bus Service No. 5

Service No. 5.—VICTORIA PARK and WINDSOR LANE travels via Cowbridge Rd., Castle St., Duke St., Queen St. and Dumphries Pl.

FROM VICTORIA PARK.		FROM WINDSOR LANE.	
Monday to Saturday.	Sunday.	Monday to Saturday.	Sunday.
a.m.	a.m.	a.m.	a.m.
7–48, 55	—	8– 3, 8, 16, 21, 26,	—
8– 1, 6, 11, 16, 21, 26,	—	31, 36, 41, 46, 51, 56	—
31, 36, 41, 46, 51, 56	—	9– 1, then every 5 or	—
9– 1, then every 5 or 6 mins. until	—	6 mins. until	—
p.m.	p.m.	p.m.	p.m.
12–43, 48, 53, 58	—	12–33, 38, 43, 48, 53, 58	—
1– 3, 8, 13, 18, 23, 28, 33, 38, 43, 48, 53, 58	1–19, 26, 34, 41, 49, 56	1– 3, 8, 13, 18, 23, 28, 33, 38, 43, 48, 53, 58	1–34, 40, 48, 55
2– 3, 8, then every 5 or 6 mins. until	and every 7 or 8 mins. until	2– 3, 8, then every 5 or 6 mins. until	and every 7 or 8 mins. until
4–35, 40, 45, 50, 55		4–33, 40, 45, 50, 55	
5– 0, 5, 10, 15, 20, 25, 30, 35, 40, 45, 50, 55		5– 0, 5, 10, 15, 20, 25, 30, 35, 40, 45, 50, 55	
6– 0, 5, 10, then every 5 or 6 mins. until		6– 0, 5, 10, then every 5 or 6 mins. until	
10– 3, 9, 14, 19, 24, 30, 35, 41, 46	10– 4, 11, 19, 26	10– 1, 6, 12, 17, 23, 28, 33, 38, 44, 49, 55*	10– 3, 10, 17, 24, 32, 41
		11– 0*	

* : Runs to Beda Road at time shown.

73.   In October 1965, a new traffic scheme was introduced which made Queen Street one-way, with traffic flowing westwards. Eastbound traffic was diverted via Kingsway, Cathays Park Road, passing the City Hall, then via Dumfries Lane and Dumfries Place. This involved re-routeing the trolleybus services and new wiring was erected by Clough, Smith and Co. Trolleybus 215 is seen on service 8 turning out of Dumfries Place into Queen Street having used the new wiring. Dumfries Place had been used as part of the Windsor Lane loop, but in the opposite direction of flow. (DG Bowen/C Taylor)

74.   The new, and very scenic, route via Cathays Park Road took trolleybuses directly past the Law Courts, City Hall and the National Museum of Wales. This is trolleybus 213 having turned into Cathays Park Road with Kingsway in the foreground and Cardiff City Hall prominent in the background. (DG Bowen/C Taylor)

QUEEN STREET TO
CASTLE STREET

75.   At the west end of Queen Street, trolleybuses on services 1, 2 and 3 turned left into St John Street.
The other services from the east proceeded forward into Duke Street. Trolleybus 227 is seen on service
4 in January 1952 passing the junction with St John Street. In the background is a trolleybus proceeding
east along Queen Street, a practice that would cease in 1965 when Queen Street became one-way.
(Photoarchives)

76.   Trolleybus 265 is on service 8 in Duke Street. Behind can be seen a service 2 trolleybus from Pengam turning into St John Street. (Photoarchives)

77.   The St John Street wiring was one-way, leading to Working Street, The Hayes and Mill Lane. It enabled services 1, 2 and 3 to reach their terminal points in St Mary Street. This link came into use on New Year's Eve 1950, replacing the routeing along Churchill Way which lasted only a short time and was unpopular with passengers. Trolleybus 255 is seen passing St John's Church on its way to St Mary Street. (DG Bowen/C Taylor)

78.   The overhead wiring junction outside Cardiff Castle at the top of the High Street was one of the most complex in Cardiff. It enabled trolleybuses to turn in any direction, as well as run straight through from Duke Street into Castle Street. The right turn from Castle Street into High Street, last regularly used by trolleybuses on service 6 until 1966, was afterwards made illegal by a traffic scheme. However the wiring was retained until the very end of the system and used on special occasions with police dispensation. This view shows single-deck trolleybus 239 turning out of High Street whilst returning to depot. These journeys were normally the only occasion that these vehicles were seen away from their usual haunt along Bute Street. In Cardiff, depot journeys were always operated in passenger service. (J White)

79.   Shown here is busy Duke Street in January 1952 looking west, the pioneer BUT trolleybus 211 passes Cardiff Castle en route for Gabalfa. The motorbus on the left is pulling out of High Street. (Photoarchives)

80.   A similar scene to the previous photograph, showing trolleybus 219 and, in the distance, a service 8 trolleybus with the full rear destination blind provision. Note the wiring connection turning left from Duke Street into High Street. This was later replaced by an interlaced wiring arrangement with the frog placed much further away from the road junction. (Photoarchives)

81.   This is a view of Castle Street looking east towards Queen Street, showing trolleybus 215, on driver training duties, approaching the High Street junction. Note the advance turnout in the wiring for the normally illegal right turn into High Street. The 'L' board in the rear window of 215 warns motorists to keep clear. (RF Mack/ Trolleybus Museum Company)

R.E.H.

CARDIFF CORPORATION TRANSPORT DEPARTMENT.

TROLLEY-BUS CONVERSION

Service No. 2—Newport Road & St. Mary St.

THE PUBLIC IS NOTIFIED THAT, COMMENCING SUNDAY, 15th OCTOBER, 1950, THE ABOVE SERVICE WILL BE REVISED AND WILL BE OPERATED BY TROLLEYBUSES TRAVELLING FROM THE GENERAL STATION, VIA WOOD ST., ST. MARY ST., HIGH ST., DUKE ST., QUEEN ST., NEWPORT RD. AND PENGAM RD. TO CLYDESMUIR RD. (present terminus of Service No. 12A/B). RETURN VIA REVERSE ROUTE TO GENERAL STATION.

CERTAIN EARLY MORNING JOURNEYS BETWEEN VICTORIA PARK AND NEWPORT RD. WHICH HAVE BEEN OPERATED HITHERTO BY MOTORBUSES, WILL BE OPERATED IN FUTURE BY TROLLEYBUSES.

FULL DETAILS OF THE NEW TIME TABLES FOR THE ABOVE SERVICES ARE SET OUT IN SERVICE PAMPHLET No. 10, AVAILABLE FROM CONDUCTORS OR FROM CENTRAL OFFICES WOOD ST., CARDIFF.

COINCIDENT WITH THE ABOVE CONVERSION, THE PRESENT TERMINUS AT CLYDESMUIR RD. FOR SERVICES No. 12 A/B—GENERAL STATION AND PENGAM, WILL BE REMOVED TO THE JUNCTION OF TWEEDSMUIR RD. AND WHITMUIR RD.   TIMETABLES FOR THIS SERVICE WILL REMAIN UNALTERED.

The PAY-AS-YOU-ENTER System will operate on Service No. 2—Pengam and St. Mary Street ONLY.

October, 1950.   J. F. SIDDALL, General Manager.

10/50 4363 EDS 4416

DOODLEBUGS AROUND MILL LANE

82.   The Bute Street service turned in the city centre using a one-way loop via Hayes Bridge Road, Mill Lane and Custom House Street. This is grey liveried ex-Pontypridd trolleybus 235 turning from Hayes Bridge Road into Mill Lane, crossing the bridge over the Glamorganshire Canal
(DF Parker)

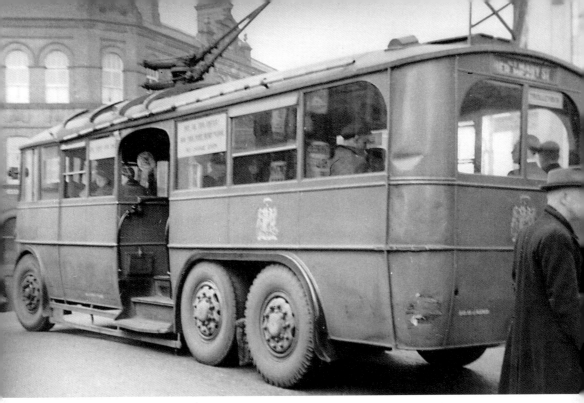

83. A closer look at trolleybus 235 turning into Mill Lane shows the central entrance and the notices about the "pay as you enter" fare collection system. (C Carter)

84. Doodlebug 234 is seen in Mill Lane. The canal ran parallel with Mill Lane behind the wall. (DA Jones / London Trolleybus Preservation Society)

85.   The original terminus of the Bute Street route was at the Monument on the canal bridge. This is trolleybus 231 at the terminus. At least two of the Doodlebugs were painted in full Cardiff livery, as seen here.
(R Marshall)

MILL LANE, MONUMENT AND ST MARY STREET

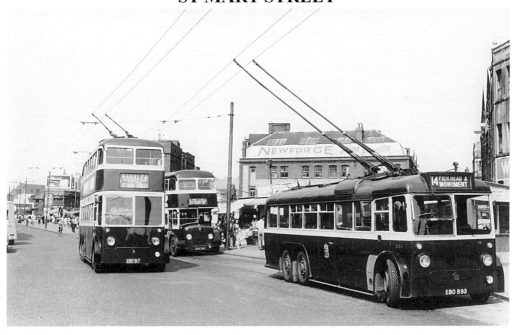

86.   For most of the life of the route, the Bute Street service terminated in the city centre in Mill Lane. By this time the canal had been built over and Mill Lane reconstructed. This animated view shows BUT single-decker 240 at the terminal stop about to be overtaken by double-decker 260, on its way to St Mary Street.
(JS King)

87.   Trolleybus 242 is seen in Custom House Street on the final part of the one-way loop before turning back into Bute Street. The overhead wiring above the opposite carriageway formed the only access for trolleybuses from Bute Street to St Mary Street and was used by depot bound workings.
(J White)

88.   This interesting photograph was taken in 1952 during the re-construction of Mill Lane. For this period, the Bute Street trolleybuses could not use their regular turning loop and were diverted via the westbound wiring in Custom House Street terminating at the Monument end of that street. This wiring was normally used for depot workings. From there, they turned using the newly constructed Monument roundabout back into Custom House Street. This view shows trolleybus 239, still with a forward exit door, turning at the Monument. Another single-decker can be seen in the background at the temporary terminal in Custom House Street. Traction poles were not allowed to be planted on the new roundabout, and this led to the Transport Department having to use 20 feet long bracket arms, for which special permission had to be sought from the Ministry of Transport. One of these can be seen behind 239. (C.Carter)

89.   Another view of the Monument roundabout showing trolleybus 221 making for St Mary Street, having come from Mill Lane, seen in the left background.
(RF Mack / Trolleybus Museum Company)

90.   A view taken in the late 1960's showing the effect of building demolition in the Monument area. Trolleybus 216 is seen, with its conductor in nonchalant pose on the platform. The wiring link from Custom House Street, seen trailing in above the vehicle, was retained as far as the feeder at the top of Bute Street for power supply purposes after the closure of the Bute Street route.
(R Marshall)

91.   The main city centre terminal stops for service 1, 2 and 3 were in St Mary Street near Wood Street. A lay-by loop was provided in the wiring to allow trolleybuses to pass each other. This scene shows trolleybus 250 departing and crossing the junction with Wood Street. In the background is another vehicle loading and the wiring loop is evident. (RF Mack / Trolleybus Museum Company)

WOOD STREET AND CENTRAL SQUARE

92.   Services 5A, 5B, 6 and 9 used the wiring connections to and from St Mary Street and Wood Street. This scene shows AEC 201 making the turn from St Mary Street on a short working 5A journey to Beda Road. This turning point was a 'round the houses' loop situated on the south side of Cowbridge Road East, mid-way between Neville Street and Victoria Park. It was dismantled in July and August 1965 following the withdrawal of the 5 group of routes. (DG Bowen/C Taylor)

93.   Wood Street was the location for the city centre loading stops for the services to Pier Head via Clarence Road and Victoria Park via Neville Street. This is AEC 206 in the 1950s loading for Pier Head alongside Central Square. (DA Jones/London Trolleybus Preservation Society)

94.   Turning facilities at Wood Street were provided by a loop around the Central Square area, circling the Central Bus Station and also passing the main entrance to Cardiff General railway station. This loop was the original turning point for the first trolleybus service in 1942, until this was extended through to Llandaff Fields later that year. In 1966, following the premature demise of the Pier Head service, trolleybuses on services 6 and 9, from Llandaff Fields and Gabalfa respectively, terminated here to allow through passengers to transfer to the replacement motorbuses. The loop lasted until the very end of the system. AEC trolleybus 204 is seen parked beside the bus station on driver training duties in July 1963. Behind is a 'Brown Bomber' Neath and Cardiff express coach. In the left background is the Wales Empire Pool, built for the Commonwealth Games in 1958 which was eventually demolished to make way for the Millennium Stadium. On the extreme left are the offices of the Corporation Transport Department. Note that 204 has had its original three-piece front destination layout replaced with the standard Cardiff one-piece rectangular arrangement. (JS King)

95.   Parked further round the loop is AEC 201, showing the distinctive rear end of this vehicle type. On the right is the frontage of Cardiff General railway station, still boldly displaying 'Great Western Railway' many years after railway nationalisation. (DG Bowen/C Taylor)

HAVELOCK STREET, WESTGATE AND CARDIFF BRIDGE

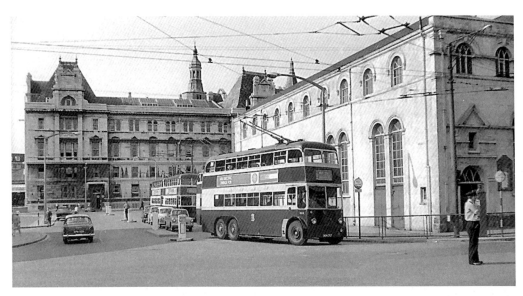

96.   The Ely service 10A and 10B terminated in Havelock Street by means of a one-way loop from Westgate via Park Street, Havelock Street and Wood Street. This is trolleybus 222 turning out of Havelock Street, commencing its journey to Ely with three other trolleybuses on the stand, an indication of the high level of service frequency. In the upper foreground can be seen the wiring from Wood Street leading into the Central Square loop. Prominent in the background is the Post Office building. Trolleybus 222 was the only one of its type to retain the front exit door throughout its life.
(RF Mack / Trolleybus Museum Company)

97. In November 1967, a new traffic scheme resulted in the direction of the loop being reversed, and the Ely service terminal being moved to the opposite side of Havelock Street. This view shows 1955 BUT 278, with poles down, possibly awaiting a crew. The new terminal arrangement, which was outside the South Wales Echo offices, is evident. Park Street is in the background. Note the 'Trolleybus' sticker on the lower deck rear window. This was intended to warn drivers of following trolleybuses not to overtake!
(Ipswich Transport Museum collection)

98.   The revised wiring arrangements necessary for the new traffic scheme included a link at the bottom of Westgate to allow depot bound trolleybuses to turn left into Wood Street. The frog and turnout for this connection is evident in this view of trolleybus 227 in Westgate Street proceeding to the Havelock Street terminal. (Ipswich Transport Museum collection)

99.   Westgate Street is a pleasant tree lined street which connected the Ely service terminal with Cowbridge Road at Cardiff Bridge. Seen near the Cardiff Bridge end is trolleybus 286 opposite the Angel Hotel. On the left can be seen the trailing frog of the wiring connection from Castle Street, used for vehicles entering service from the depot. Cardiff Arms Park rugby ground was on the left. (RF Mack / Trolleybus Museum Company)

100. Looking in the opposite direction from the previous photograph, this view shows trolleybus 218 entering Westgate Street from Cardiff Bridge, followed by a Rhondda AEC bus. The wiring link from Castle Street is evident. (RFMack/Trolleybus Museum Company)

101. On the western edge of the city centre, trolleybuses crossed the River Taff at Cardiff Bridge, another of the system's beauty spots. Trolleybus 258, looking rather battered, is seen leaving the bridge on a journey along Cowbridge Road to Ely. (RF Mack / Trolleybus Museum Company)

DEPOTS

←————— 102.   The initial trolleybus fleet was housed at Clare Road tram depot, which dated from 1902 and was situated on the western side of the city, on the pioneer Clarence Road trolleybus route. The depot was shared with trams until 1946. Trolleybuses entered at the front of the building from Clare Road and came out at the rear into Pendyris Street, which ran along the side of the building. From 1947, the depot housed the single-deck fleet for the Bute Street route. This is a view from the depot entrance looking towards Clare Road, which runs across the background. There were wiring connections to and from the Clarence Road and city centre directions. Seen here is ex-Pontypridd trolleybus 231 entering the depot, followed by two BUT double-deckers on 15th March 1950. (IL Wright)

103.   This is Pendyris Street alongside Clare Road depot, showing a line-up of trolleybuses headed by 266. Note one of the BUT single-deckers in the far distance. The depot generally operated vehicles for the western routes, but closed from 25th October 1953 when all trolleybus operations were transferred to Roath Depot. (RWA Jones/Online Photo Archive/Photobus)

104.   Roath Depot was in Newport Road at the eastern edge of the city and near the terminus of the Pengam trolleybus route. Adjacent to the site was the power station that originally supplied the power for the tramway. It commenced trolleybus operation when the eastern routes began to be converted from trams in 1949. Originally it accommodated vehicles from the eastern trolleybus routes, but from 1953, after the closure of Clare Road Depot, it housed the whole fleet. All trolleybus overhauls took place here. From 1950 it was purely a trolleybus depot, a situation that lasted until the conversion of trolleybus routes to motorbuses commenced - diesel buses being allocated from 1963. Trolleybus 286 is seen here about to enter the depot. Only the most easterly arch was used by trolleybuses, the other three being bricked-up. (RF Mack / Trolleybus Museum Company)

105.   On the western side of the building, there was a large open-air parking area for the fleet. Single–deck trolleybus 238 is prominent in this view. (RF Mack / Trolleybus Museum Company)

106.   All engineering work on the vehicles was carried out at Roath Depot. This unusual view shows trolleybus 273 receiving attention to its underside. (DG Bowen/C Taylor)

107.   This is a glimpse into the depot building in July 1950, showing one of the ancillary vehicles associated with the trolleybuses. UH 9004 was a traction pole carrier and was based on a 1931 Thorneycroft bus chassis which was until 1945 No.135 in the Cardiff motorbus fleet. In the background is a line of brand new BUT double-deck trolleybuses awaiting entry into service. The rear-most one is 267, showing a destination blind for service 12 from Roath Dock to St Mary Street. This route was planned but never came to fruition. (IL Wright)

108.   201 to 210 CKG 191 to 200
The chassis contract for the initial ten trolleybuses had originally been awarded to Leyland Motors, but this was frustrated by their involvement in war work. Instead, the work was given to AEC of Southall, who supplied their 664T three-axle chassis, the last of this type to be built. The 70 seat rear-entrance bodywork was by Northern Counties of Wigan, a regular supplier to Cardiff before the war, and these were the only trolleybus bodies built by the company. Special Cardiff requirements required the completed vehicle to be built to a low height of 15 feet and able to withstand flood water of up to 8 inches. Five of them entered service on 1st March 1942 and most of the remainder in November 1942, when the initial route was extended to Llandaff Fields. They were all originally painted in wartime grey livery. After the war, at least three (204, 208, 209) were painted in a very striking streamlined version of the Cardiff crimson-lake and cream colours. This was a very short-lived arrangement and all the vehicles subsequently had the standard livery. Later in their life, some had their three-piece destination indicators replaced with the standard single rectangular aperture. 208 was lavishly decorated to celebrate Cardiff's fifty years as a city in 1955, although it did not run in public service in this form. Later, some of this batch were regularly decorated with coloured lamps (see photograph 115). The first withdrawals occurred in 1962, although 201, 202, 204 and 207 lasted until 1965. This is 208 in the short-lived streamlined livery posed at the entrance to Clare Road depot. Note the pay as you enter signs in the lower-deck windows and the identification light adjacent to the front destination indicator. (English Electric/C Taylor collection)

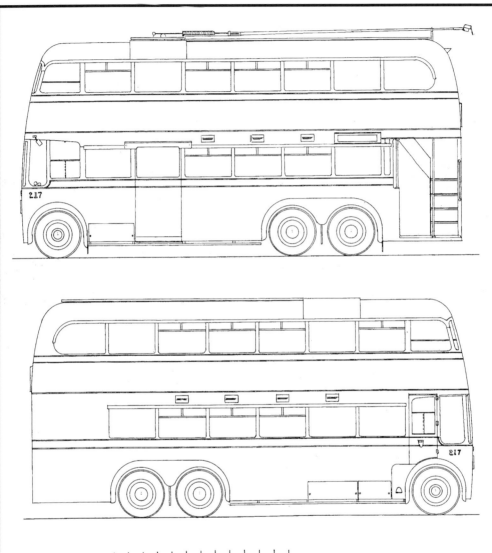

CARDIFF CORPORATION
3 AXLE D/DECK TROLLEYBUS

Body: East Lancs. 1948 Chassis: BUT 9641T. Fleet No. 211 –229.	Scale: 4 mm = 1Foot.

DRAWING No. TB52

109.   **231 to 237   TG 379, 381, 383, 385, 387, 389, 391**
Purchased to convert the Bute Street service to trolleybus operation, these seven second-hand vehicles came from nearby Pontypridd Urban District Council in 1947. They were centre-entrance 32 seaters built by English Electric in 1930, and had operated entirely on Pontypridd's one route system. Known as 'Doodlebugs', these vehicles were decidedly old-fashioned, being slow and noisy. They also had obsolete Estler trolleybases, with the trolleys mounted on top of each other. Most were painted in the wartime grey livery, although at least two (231 and 236) entered service in the full Cardiff colours and some of the others later gained this livery. Always intended to have a short life in Cardiff, they were replaced by new BUT single-deckers in 1949, although a trio (231, 234 and 236) lingered on until 1950. 236 is seen outside Clare Road depot on 23rd April 1950. (AE Old)

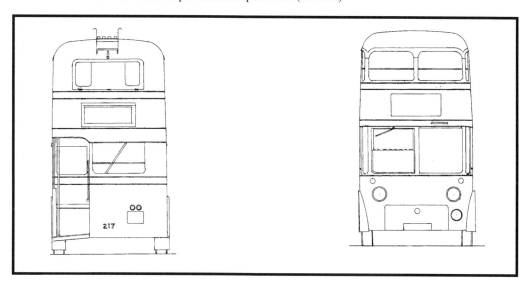

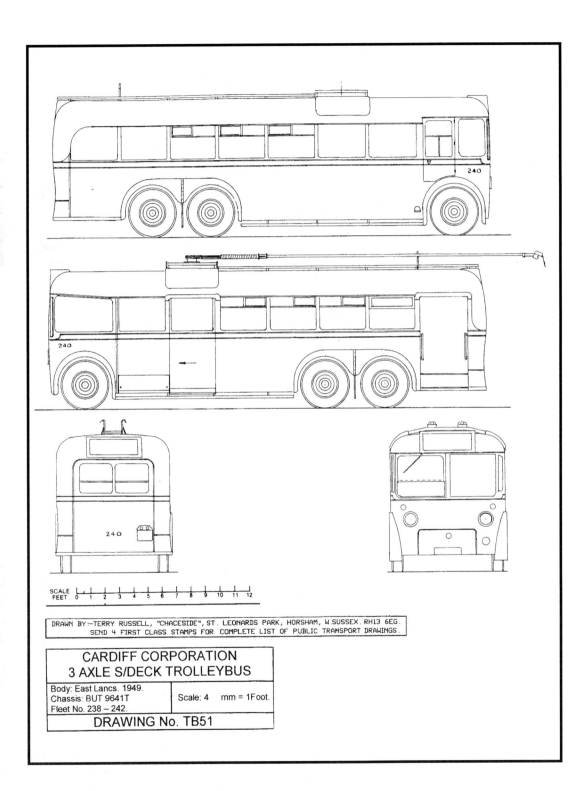

SCALE
FEET 0 1 2 3 4 5 6 7 8 9 10 11 12

DRAWN BY:—TERRY RUSSELL, "CHACESIDE", ST. LEONARDS PARK, HORSHAM, W.SUSSEX. RH13 6EG.
SEND 4 FIRST CLASS STAMPS FOR COMPLETE LIST OF PUBLIC TRANSPORT DRAWINGS.

CARDIFF CORPORATION
3 AXLE S/DECK TROLLEYBUS

Body: East Lancs. 1949. Chassis: BUT 9641T Fleet No. 238 – 242.	Scale: 4 mm = 1Foot.

DRAWING No. TB51

110. 211 to 230, 245 to 247, 249, 250 DBO 471 to 480, DUH 716 to 725, EBO 902 to 904, 906,907

These 25 vehicles had BUT 9641T chassis with eight-feet-wide East Lancashire 67-seat bodies and were part of the large order for 70 double-deck trolleybuses placed after the war. Fifty from this order were delivered between 1948 and 1950. The bodies were designed jointly by the Cardiff Chief Engineer and East Lancashire Coachbuilders of Blackburn to a design that facilitated the "pay as you enter"

fare collection scheme. It incorporated two staircases, an air-operated sliding exit door as well as a rear platform entrance with a space for a conductor's seat. East Lancs built the whole of the bodies on this batch of 25, and the remainder, were sent elsewhere for completion as detailed in the next photograph. Even so the final five of these pure East Lancs vehicles (245 to 247, 249, 250) were constructed at the coachbuilder's Bridlington subsidiary. Despite their special design features, they did not operate for long in their intended mode, the "pay as you enter" fare scheme being discontinued in late 1950. After this, the front exit doors were not used and gradually panelled over, although 222 retained this feature throughout its life. Many of the vehicles were subsequently modified with rebuilt upper-deck front windows and destination glasses. Withdrawals commenced in 1965, but Nos. 215, 218, 220 and 227 survived until the end of the system. This view of trolleybus 230 when new alongside Clare Road depot shows the typical East Lancs front dome with valances over the front upper deck windows.
(RF Mack collection / Trolleybus Museum Society)

111. 248, 251 to 274 EBO 905, 908 to 921, FBO 85 to 94.

The remaining 25 BUT trolleybuses from this 50 vehicle delivery had their bodywork constructed by a local Cardiff firm, Bruce Coachworks of Pengam Airport, using East Lancashire frames. Visually, they could be distinguished by their squarer front domes and shallower valances over the upper deck front windows. The vehicle interior also lacked the refinement of the East Lancs bodies, with poorer quality woodwork. The first to be completed was 264, which entered service in November 1949. The last of the batch entered service in late 1950 and were therefore hardly used in "pay as you enter" form. 272 was fitted with railway-type sliding opening windows and 263 was fitted for a short period in 1960 with trolley retrievers, an experiment that proved unsuccessful. The service history of these vehicles largely mirrored

that of the East Lancs batch and the first withdrawal was 260 in 1965. All were withdrawn by early 1969, although 262, which was preserved privately, returned to service (with its exit door restored) for the closure ceremony and, appropriately for a Welsh built vehicle, became Cardiff's last trolleybus. This is a view of 264, 'the first trolleybus built in Wales' in its later life leaving Gabalfa terminus, having been fitted with a modernised destination glass. (AB Cross)

112.   238 to 242 EBO 891 to 895
Five BUT 9641T chassis with East Lancashire single-deck rear–entrance 38 seat bodies were delivered
in 1949 to replace the seven ex-Pontypridd vehicles. Although they were modern vehicles with a lively
performance, unlike their predecessors, they inherited their nickname and were known as 'doodlebugs'
throughout their life. They were essentially a single-deck version of the contemporary double-deckers
including a forward exit door although the rear platform was enclosed. Perhaps because of this, they
had a reputation for being slow at loading passengers, which was definitely a disadvantage on such a
busy and short route. Like the double-deckers, the exit doors were subsequently panelled over. For their
whole life they operated on the Bute Street service and all were withdrawn upon the closure of that route
in January 1964. A smart looking 238, the first of the batch, is seen here in Mill Lane early in its life.
(DA Jones / London Trolleybus Preservation Society)

113.   275 to 287 KBO 948 to 960

The extension of the trolleybus service to the Ely housing scheme in 1955 required the purchase of thirteen additional double-deck trolleybuses. Interestingly, these came from the original order for 75 BUT vehicles that was placed just after the war, and of which 55, including five single-deckers, had been delivered between 1948 and 1950. Again BUT 9641T chassis were supplied with East Lancashire bodywork. On this occasion, the body design was more conventional as the special features for "pay as you enter" operation were not required, allowing the seating capacity to be increased to 72. All these vehicles lasted until the final years of the system, the first withdrawal being 280 in October 1968. 277 received a rebuilt upper deck front following an accident in 1968. These were particularly handsome vehicles, as shown here in this view of 280 in Havelock Street. (S Lockwood collection)

114.   243 KBO 961

Entering service in 1955 at the same time as the thirteen double–deckers was this additional single-decker, bought to provide a spare vehicle for the Bute Street service. This was a modernised version of the previous single deckers, and it had the same combination of BUT chassis and East Lancs body. It was numbered 243, partly filling the gap of two fleet numbers which followed on from the earlier single-deckers. There never was a trolleybus numbered 244. Its service life was short, being withdrawn at the closure of the Bute Steet route in 1964. Of the large post-war 75 vehicle order, this was the last and 69th vehicle. The remaining 6 chassis were mutually cancelled by the operator and manufacturer. This unique vehicle, the last three-axle single-deck trolleybus built for British use, is seen at Pier Head when new. It was acquired for preservation, and is currently being restored by the Cardiff and South Wales Trolleybus Project. (S Lockwood collection)

ILLUMINATIONS

115. Cardiff was probably unique in that during the 1960s, some of its trolleybuses were routinely decorated with illuminated lamps during November and December. The practice started in 1962 for the Cardiff Shopping Week, followed by Christmas, and for the next three years until 1964, several of the AEC vehicles (which were 6 inches narrower than the other trolleybuses) were illuminated each year with lights and fibreglass decorations on the front and sides. This view shows AEC 202 in St Mary Street attracting the attention of passers-by. All such decorated trolleybuses operated in normal service. (DG Bowen/CTaylor)

116. Following the withdrawal of the last of the AECs, in 1965, a few BUT vehicles were illuminated each Christmas until 1968. However, because of their greater width, the decorations were confined to the fronts of the vehicles only. This very seasonal 1967 view shows trolleybus 262 turning into Havelock Street from Wood Street using the recently revised terminal loop for the Ely services. (DG Bowen/CTaylor)

ON TOUR

117. During the latter years of the Cardiff trolleybus system, the Transport Department allowed some owners of preserved trolleybuses from other systems to operate private tours with their vehicle. One of the more unusual vehicles to appear was Bournemouth 202, a Sunbeam MS2 with open-top bodywork. This operated two tours in October 1969 and is seen passing under the railway bridge in Newport Road near the depot. It is to be hoped that the upper-deck passengers kept to their seats during this manoeuvre. (DG Bowen/C Taylor).

FINALE

118. Due to industrial action by the Transport Department's engineering staff, the last trolleybuses operating in normal service ran unexpectedly on Wednesday 3rd December 1969, trolleybus 286 being the very last. However, arrangements were well advanced for the final closure ceremonies, and these took place during the week commencing 5th January 1970. The proceedings were co-ordinated by trolleybus enthusiast organisations, principally the Cardiff Trolleybus Society, the Maypine Trolleybus Company and the National Trolleybus Association and no formal civic ceremony was planned. One further complication was that the wiring across Ely Bridge had been removed due to the bridge works there. On the final weekend, private tours were operated and these managed to gain access to the outer end of the Ely service by being towed across Ely Bridge. This view shows trolleybus 277 undergoing this manoeuvre on the final day, Sunday 11th January. (DF Parker)

MAYPINE TROLLEYBUS Co.

*Special Trolleybus Tour during the
Last Day of Electric Trolleybus Operation
in the City of Cardiff*

Sunday, 11th January, 1970

Convey _S. LOCKWOOD._ Seat _34_ Car _A._

Depart		To be
Roath Garage		shown on
10.15 a.m.	Event "F"	demand.

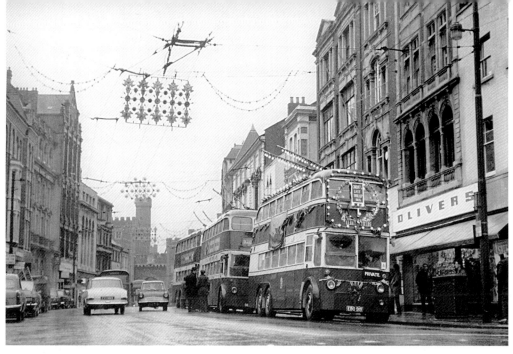

119. Trolleybus 262, already owned by the Cardiff Trolleybus Society, was hired back to the Transport Department for the week and was suitably decorated and illuminated in typical Cardiff fashion. It operated a special public service from Wood Street to Victoria Park and Roath Depot, then returning to Wood Street. On Friday and Saturday 9th and 10th January, a more intensive public service operated between Havelock Street and Victoria Park using Cardiff's own trolleybuses. This is the scene on the final day, Sunday 11th January when the three trolleybuses engaged on private tours lined up in High Street. Behind decorated 262 are 215 and 277.
(RD Hellyar-Symonds)

120. The tour trolleybuses left Victoria Park in convoy, with 262 in the rear, at 4pm for the final run to Roath Depot. This is 262, draped in the Welsh flag, entering Roath Depot for the final time – the last six-wheel trolleybus to operate on British roads. Shortly afterwards the power was switched off and Cardiff's trolleybus era was finally over.
(DG Bowen/C Taylor)

MP Middleton Press

EVOLVING THE ULTIMATE RAIL ENCYCLOPEDIA

Easebourne Lane, Midhurst, West Sussex.
GU29 9AZ   Tel:01730 813169

www.middletonpress.co.uk   email:info@middletonpress.co.uk
A-0 906520   B-1 873793   C-1 901706   D-1 904474

OOP Out of Print at time of printing - Please check current availability   **BROCHURE AVAILABLE SHOWING NEW TITLES**